To Mom, Dad and my Bens for your endless support for both my writing and my ever-present itch to buy a plane ticket.

The Traveler's Treasures

Copyright © 2021 Elaina Doeden

All rights reserved. No part of this publication may be reproduced, distributed, or transmitted in any form or by any means, including photocopying, recording, or other electronic or mechanical methods, without the prior written permission of the publisher, except in the case of brief quotations embodied in critical reviews and certain other noncommercial uses permitted by copyright law.

ISBN: 978-0-9984480-6-0

Libray of Congress: 2021906388

Names, characters, and places are products of the author's imagination.
Front cover image, illustrations, and book design by Stefanie Geyer.
Printed in the United States of America by Bang Printing.
First printing edition 2021.

Published by Rodney K Press
RodneyKPress.com

Follow the Author Elaina Doeden on Instagram
@Elainajoydoe

Follow the Illustrator Stefanie Geyer on Instagram
@Stefanie_taylor_art

The Traveler's Treasures

-WRITTEN BY-
ELAINA DOEDEN

-ILLUSTRATED BY-
STEFANIE GEYER

If I had to wave goodbye and travel far away,

On train rides through towering mountains

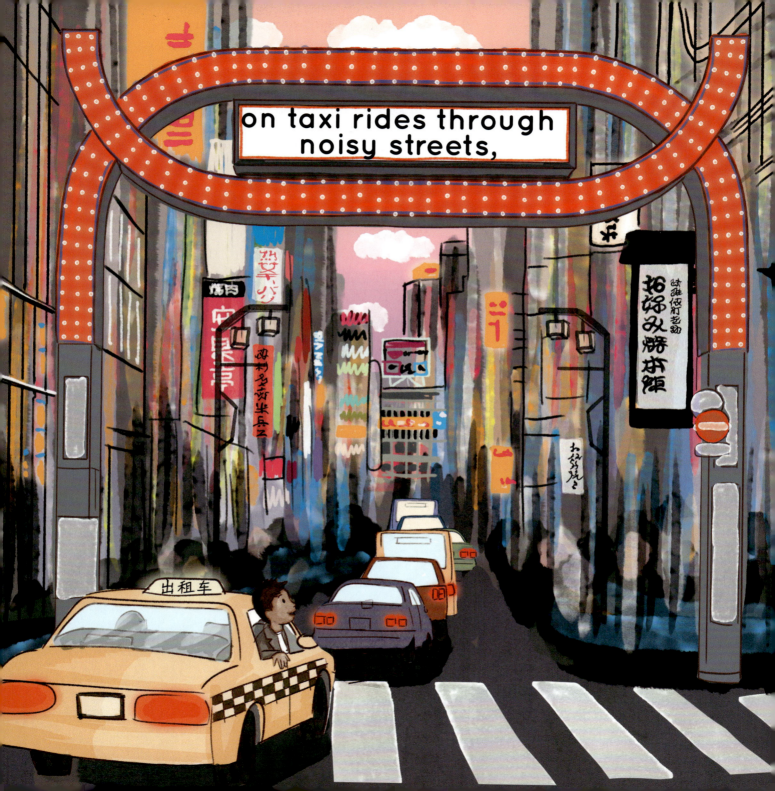

I would stroll through vibrant Nyhavn Harbor and wrap Raclette in a napkin from the Christmas markets.

It would likely spoil on the journey home, so I would be sure to tell you just how delicious it was.

I would scale the giant Sequoias to pick a seed for your garden.

I would dive into crystal waters off the coast of South Australia to meet my first new friend and haul an astonishing gift up to the surface from his cave of pearly whites.

I would turn cartwheels along the Great Wall of China and balance one of its ancient bricks atop the teetering tooth.

I would trudge through snowy wilderness and howling winds to coax an iceberg out of its shivering waters.

I would gallop through the African grasslands until I spotted the majestic long-legged creature slurping leaves for her lunch. If she became my second new friend and fancied the voyage, she would accompany me to my final destination.

The journey home would feel like years and years, as I would be exhausted from my excursions and all the more eager to greet you and unload my pack.

For all the excitement, the treasures, and the sights of the world could not for a moment compare to the joy I have in my heart when I see you.

Because the only way you can truly experience the wonders of this world is if, one day, you go explore it yourself . . .

ABOUT THE AUTHOR

Elaina began her first book when she was eight years old in a journal her grandma gave her to "write all of her stories in." She is passionate about travel and studied abroad in London in 2018. While she has traveled to a few of the places in this book, she is eager to one day visit them all. Elaina lives in Mankato, Minnesota with her husband, Ben, and their Australian Shepherd, Winnie.

Follow Elaina on Instagram @Elainajoydoe

Photo by Madelyn Rasmussen

ABOUT THE ILLUSTRATOR

Stefanie is a children's book illustrator from Winamac, Indiana. She began her art training at a young age attending drawing classes with her mother. She loves traveling the United States and would love to travel to other countries one day. She lives with her boyfriend Chris and their five dogs Halen, Presley, Kimber, Roux, and Draco.

To see more of Stefanie's work, follow her on Instagram @Stefanie_Taylor_Art.